YOU ARE BRAVE

By Chelsey Chapeau
Illustrated by Jacqueline Kriebel

In honor of
my son Grayson Chapeau
& in loving memory of
Kamryn Schumacher

YOU ARE A SUPERHERO

PHILIPPIANS 4:13

YOU ARE COURAGEOUS

JOSHUA 1:9 & ZEPHANIAH 3:17

WHEN YOU FACE THE UNKNOWN.

YOU ARE PATIENT

ROMANS 8:25

WHEN YOU WAIT FOR THE DOCTOR.

YOU ARE FEARLESS

2 TIMOTHY 1:7 & PSALM 112:7-8

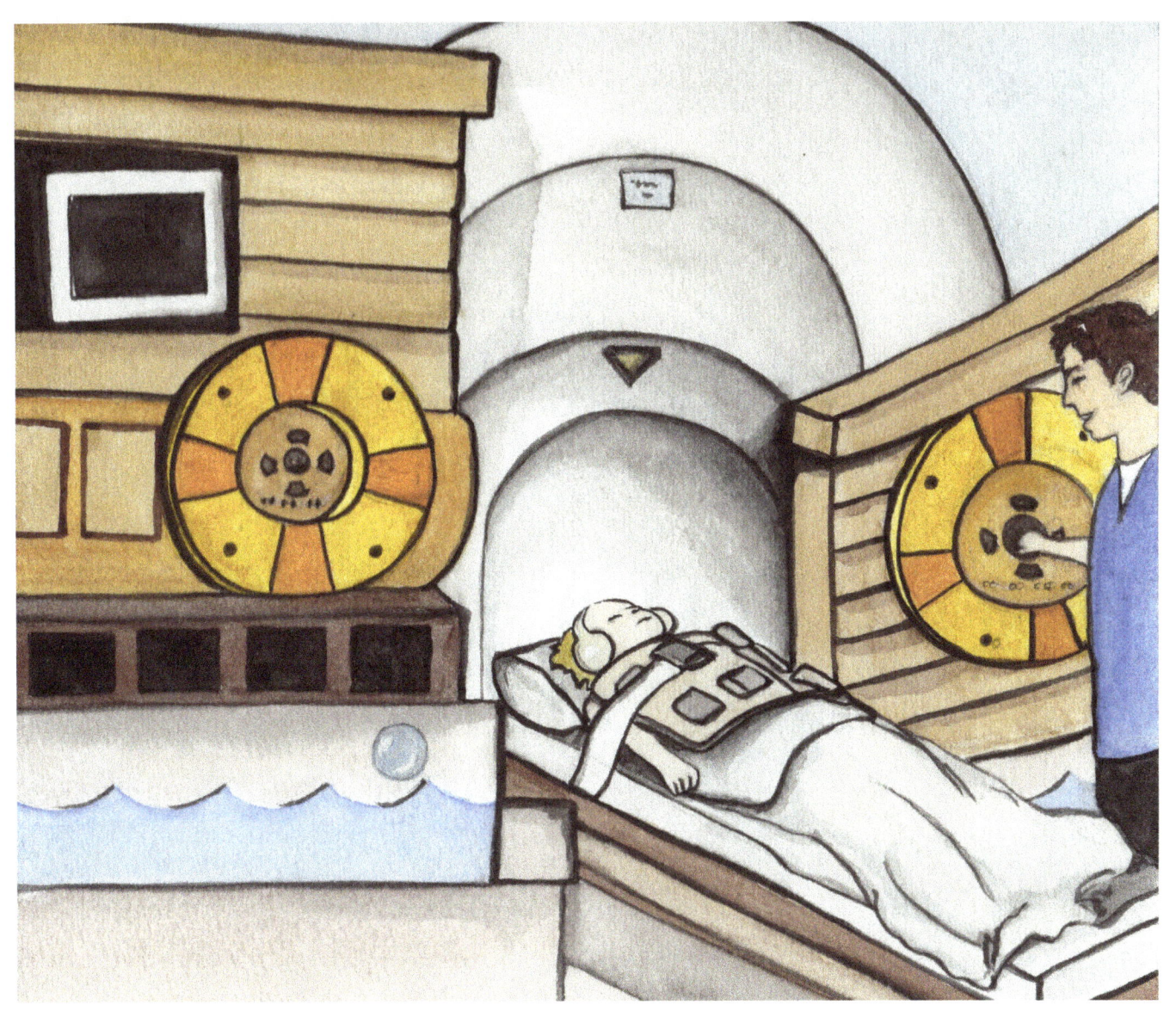

WHEN YOU TRY HARD THINGS.

YOU ARE BRAVE

ISAIAH 41:10 & ROMANS 8:38-39

EVEN IF YOU FEEL AFRAID.

YOU ARE JOYFUL

HABAKKUK 3:17-19 & ROMANS 15:13

WHEN YOU SMILE,
EVEN IF YOU DON'T FEEL GOOD.

YOU ARE STRONG

ISAIAH 40:27-31 & PSALM 46:1

EVEN IF YOU NEED HELP.

YOU ARE KIND

LUKE 6:31

WHEN YOU SHARE YOUR JOURNEY WITH A NEW FRIEND.

YOU ARE TOUGH

MATTHEW 11:28-30 & PSALM 73:26

EVEN IF YOU FEEL WEAK.

YOU ARE BEAUTIFUL

PSALM 139:1-18

EVEN IF YOU LOSE YOUR HAIR.

BUT, NO MATTER WHAT...

PSALM 23:1-6

In loving memory of Kamryn Schumacher,
who adored bubbles, a special blue bubble
has been hidden within each image.
Can you find them?